Nicknames
for
Abraham Lincoln

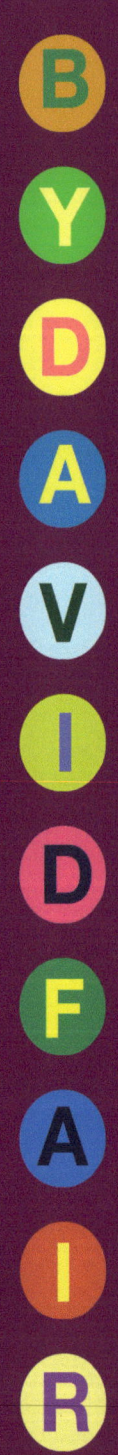

Nicknames For Abraham Lincoln Alphabet

By David Fair

With Illustrations By Ms. Martin's
4th Grade Class,
Sandymount Elementary School

ShakeMore Publishing

NICKNAMES FOR ABRAHAM LINCOLN ALPHABET

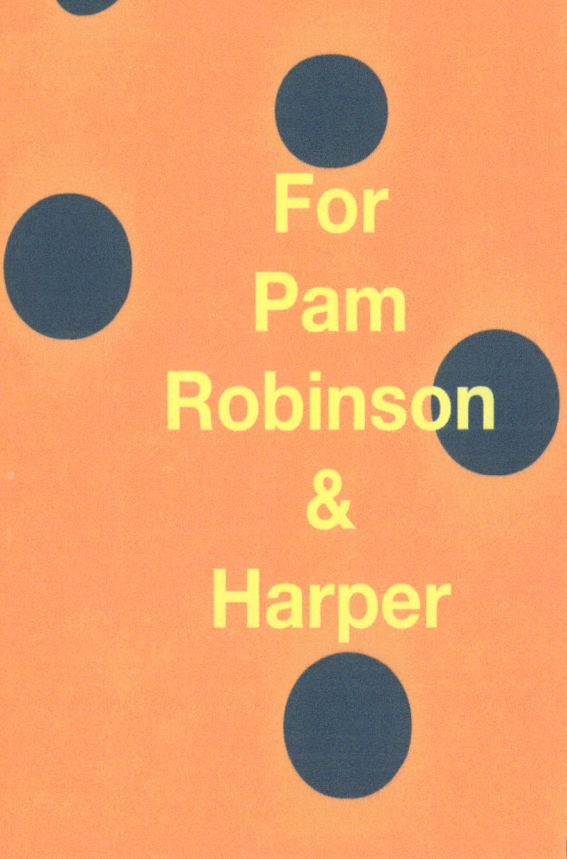

For
Pam
Robinson
&
Harper

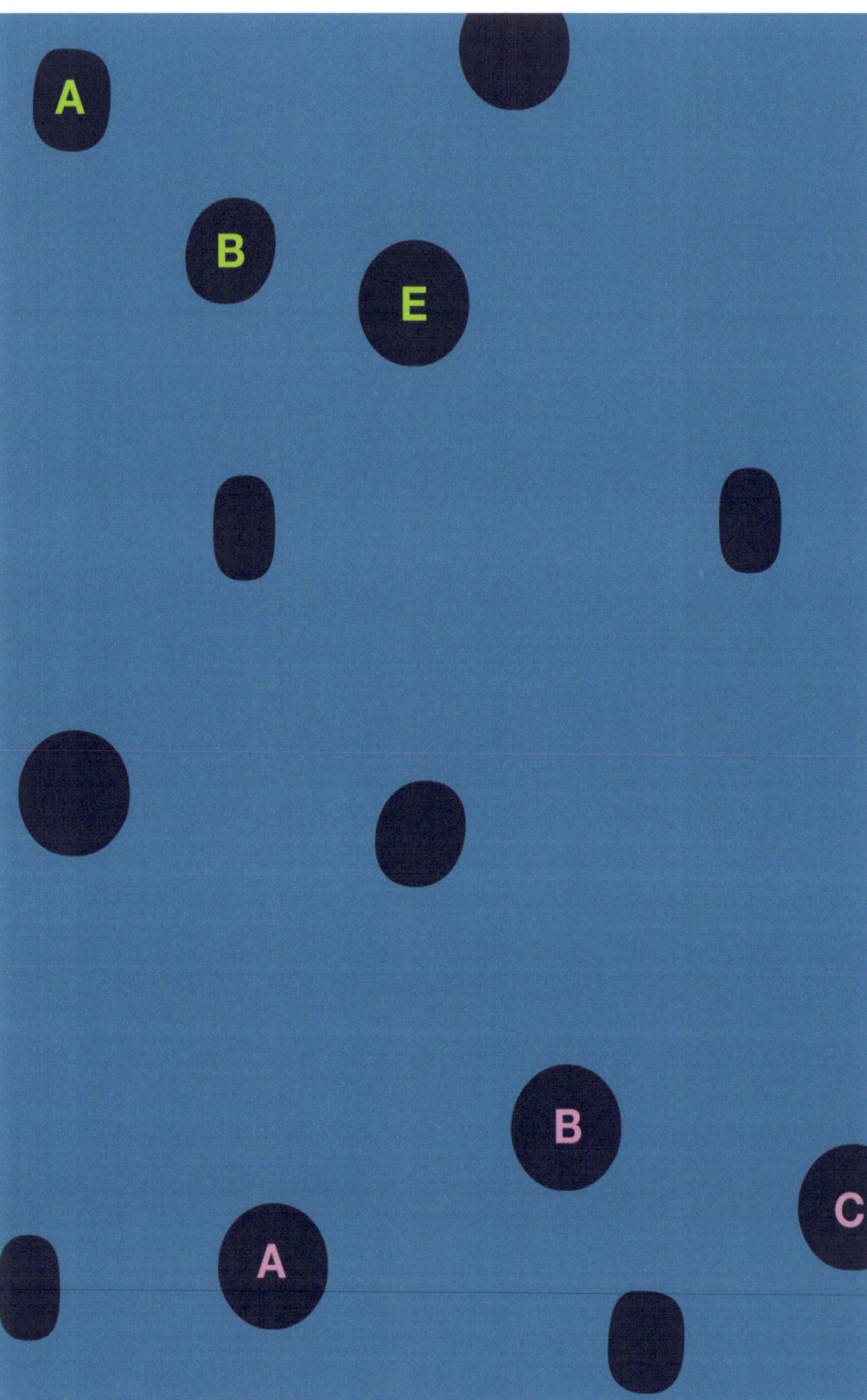

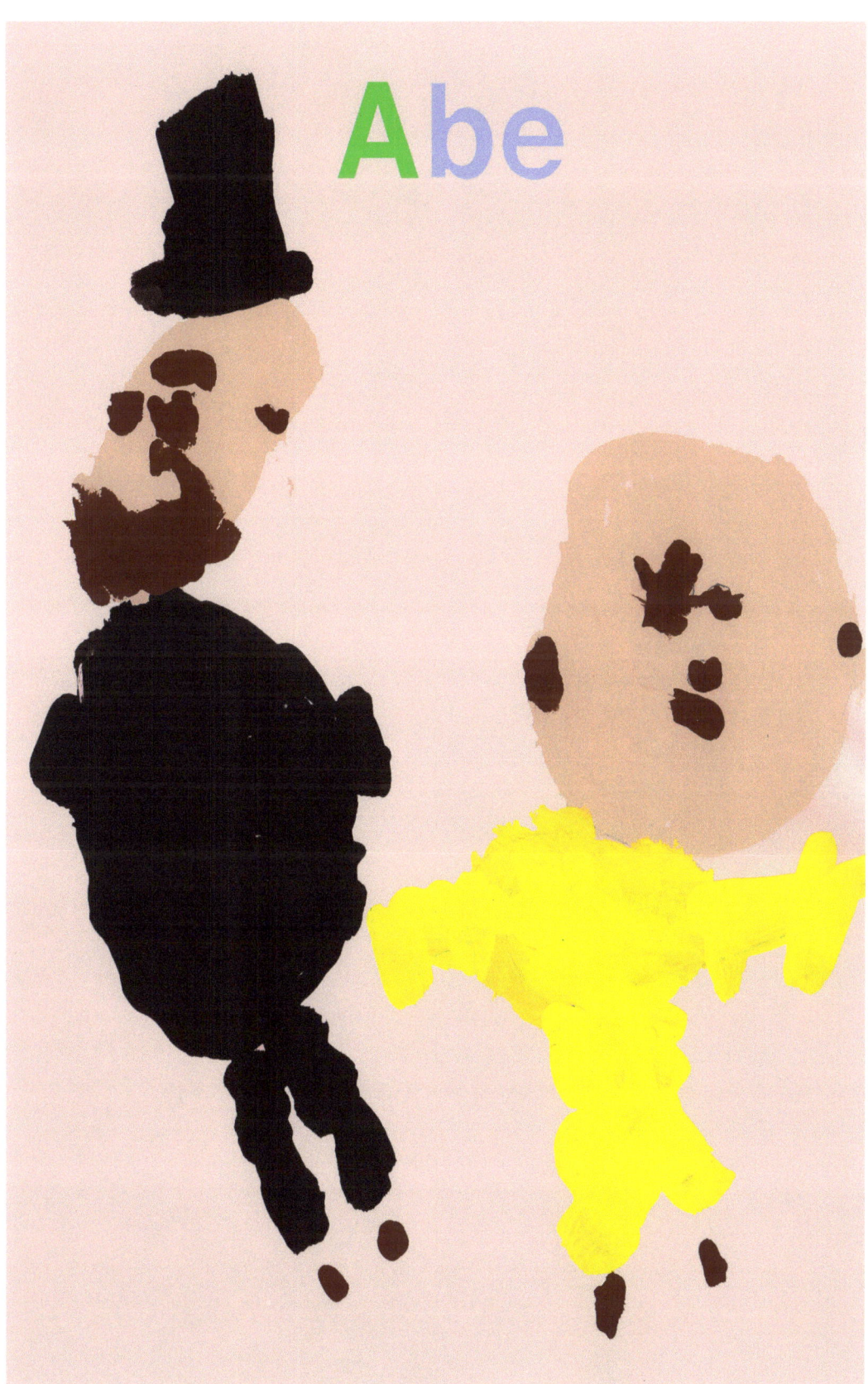

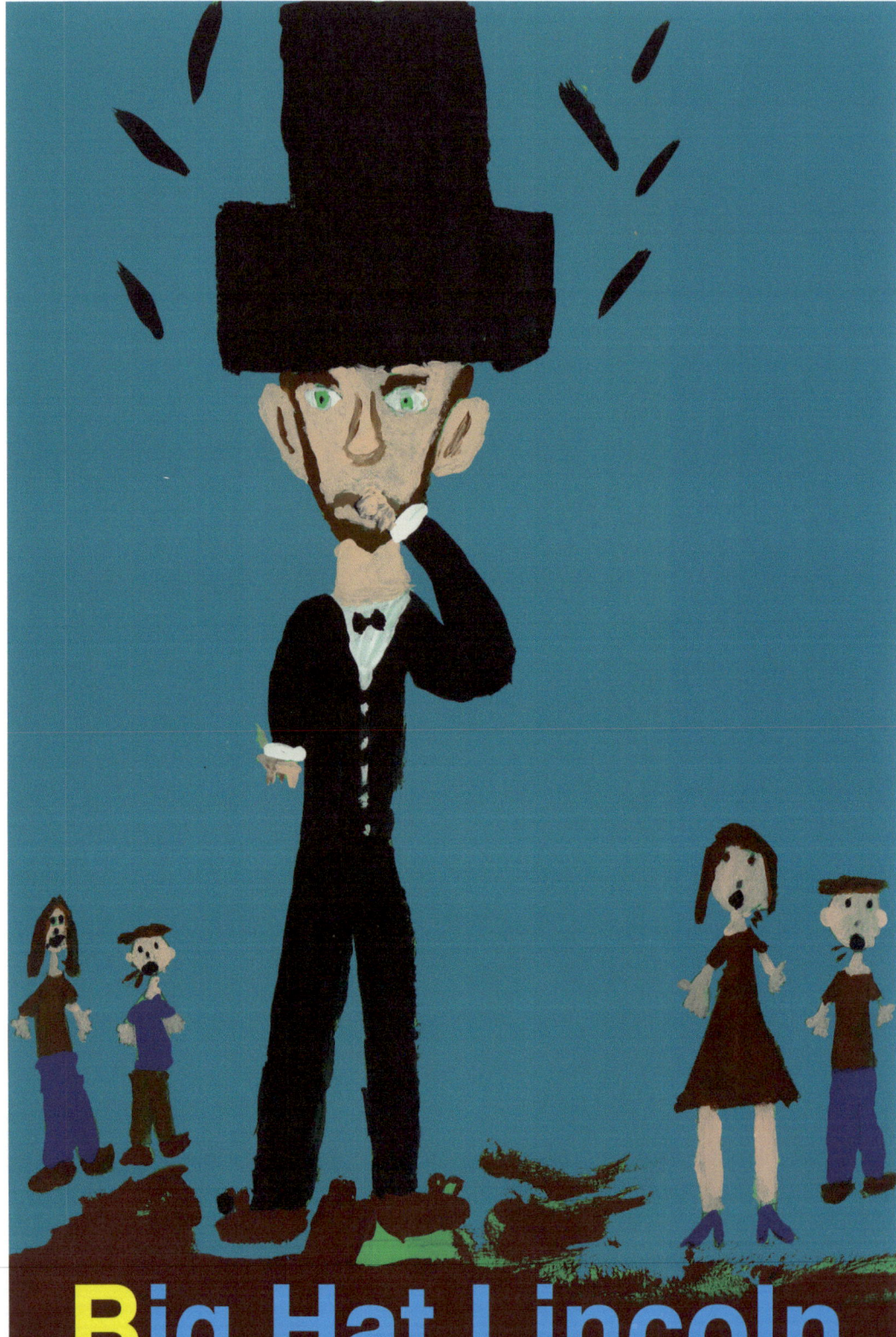

Big Hat Lincoln

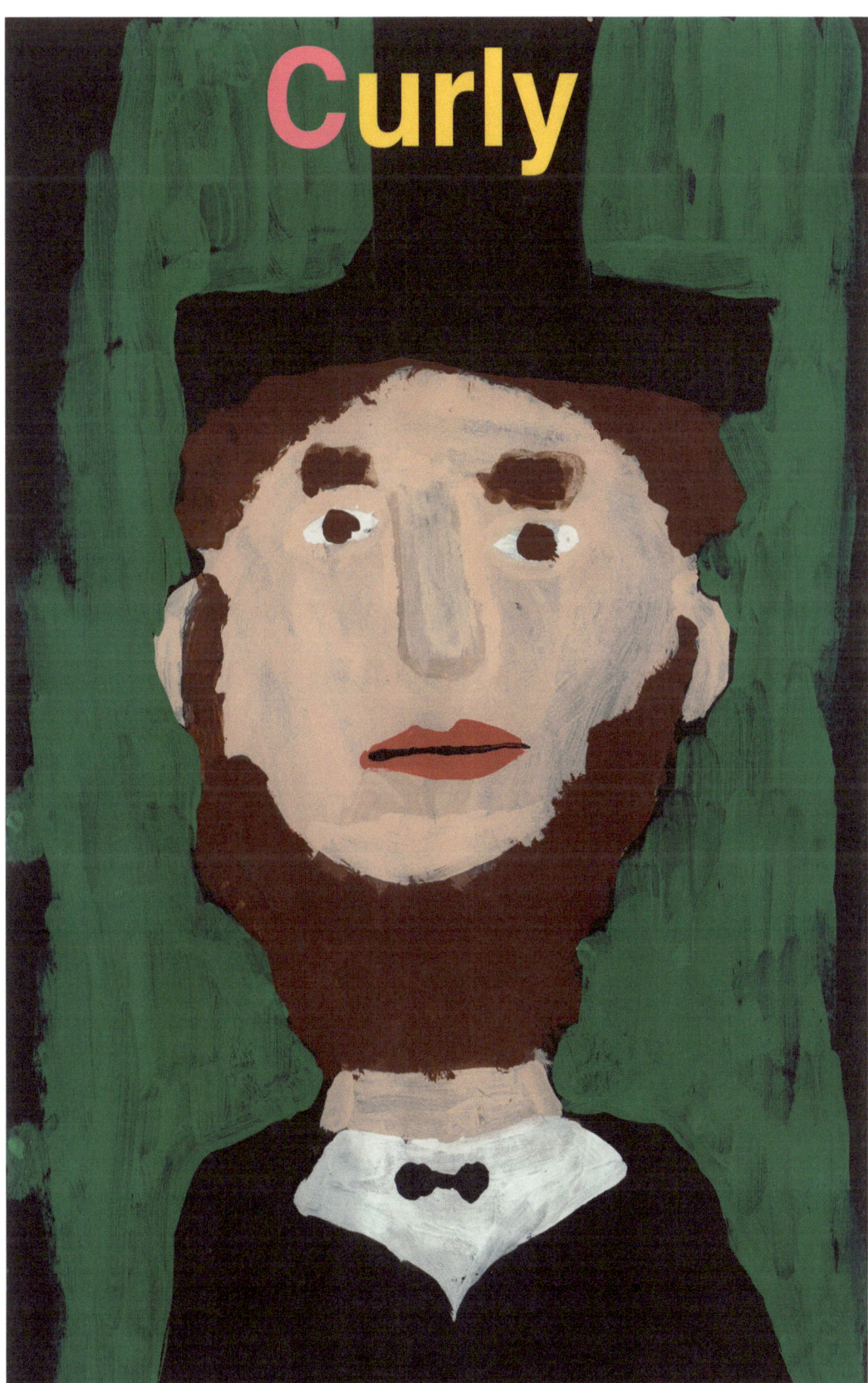

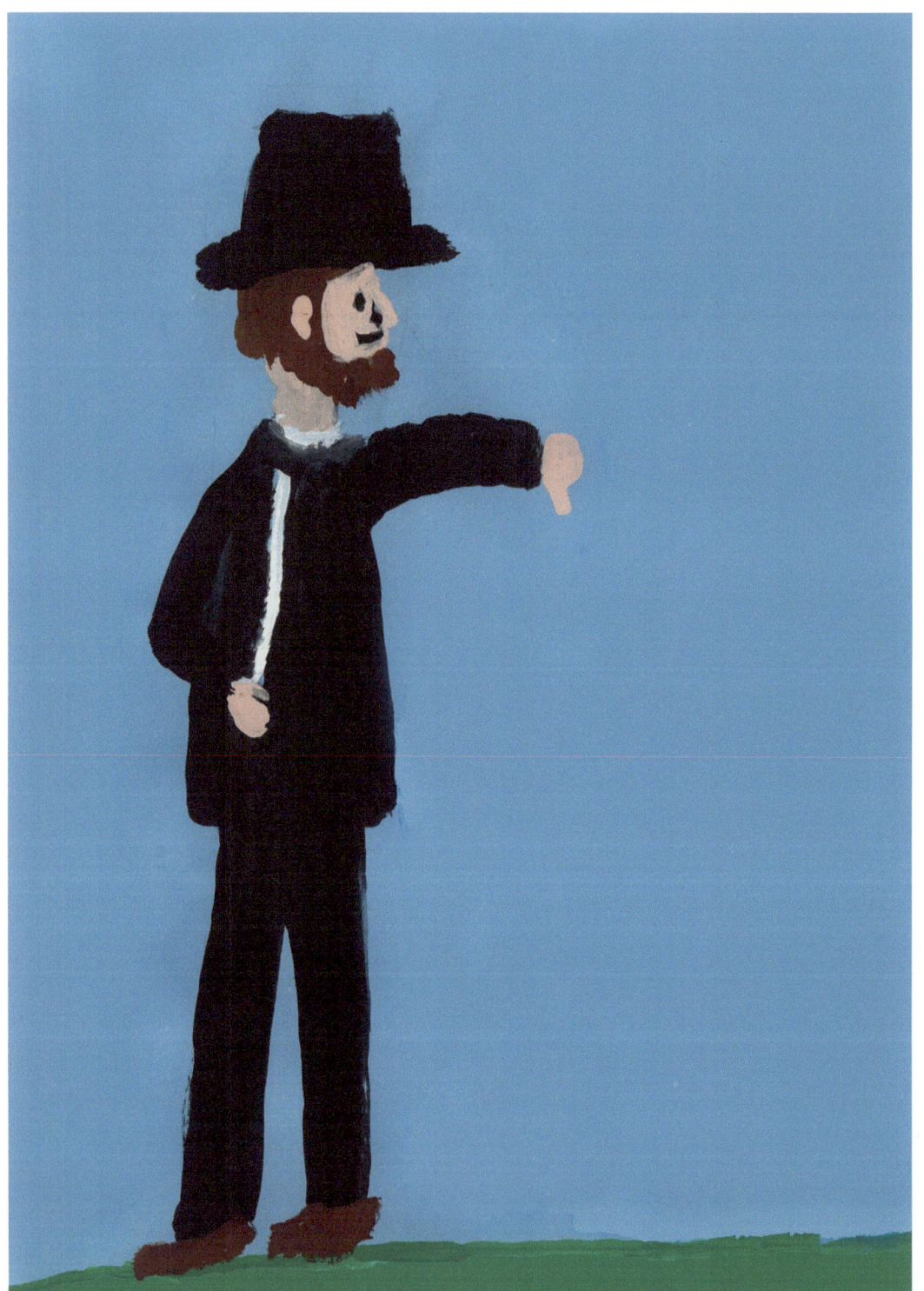

Debate King

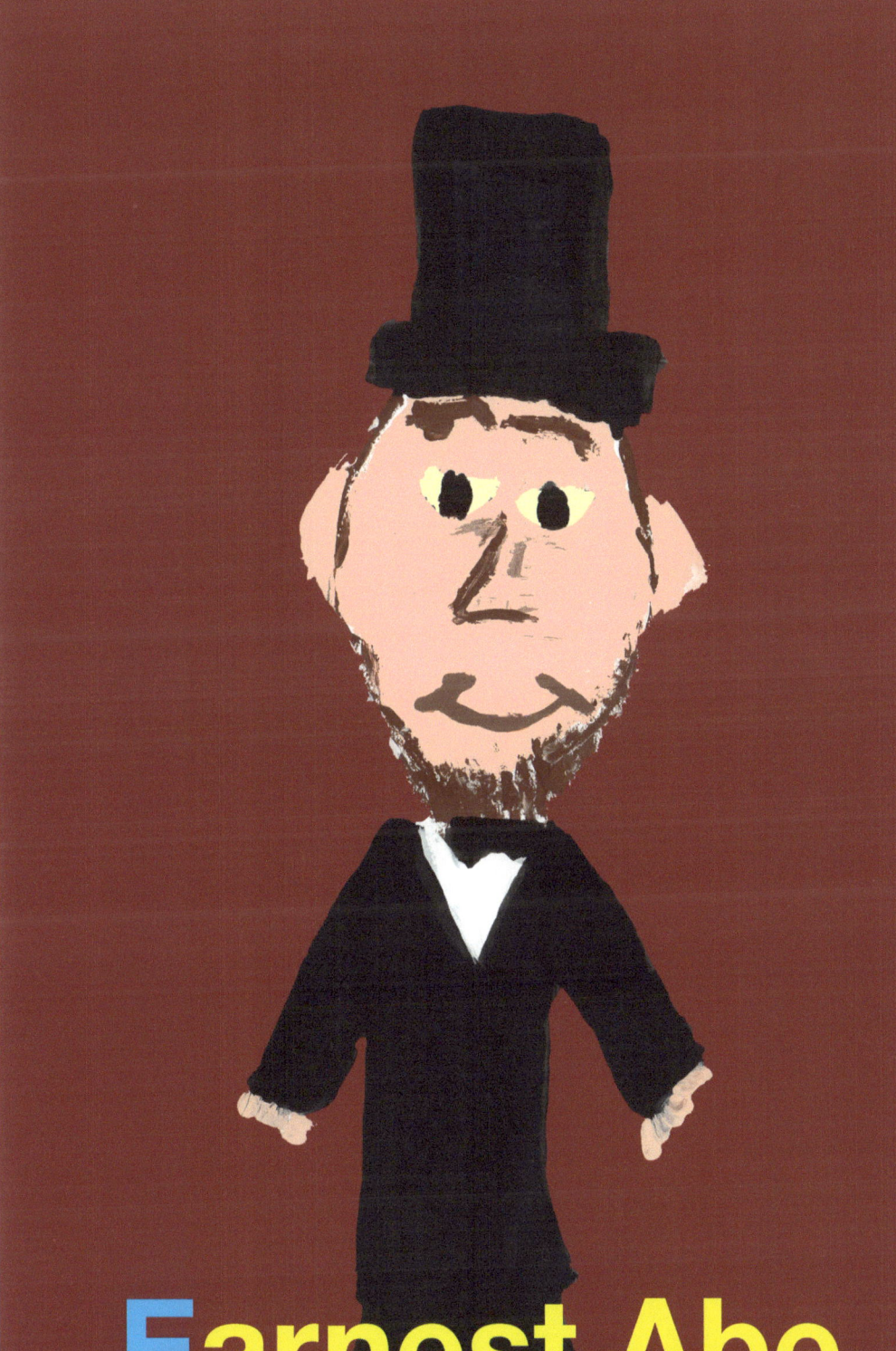

Earnest Abe

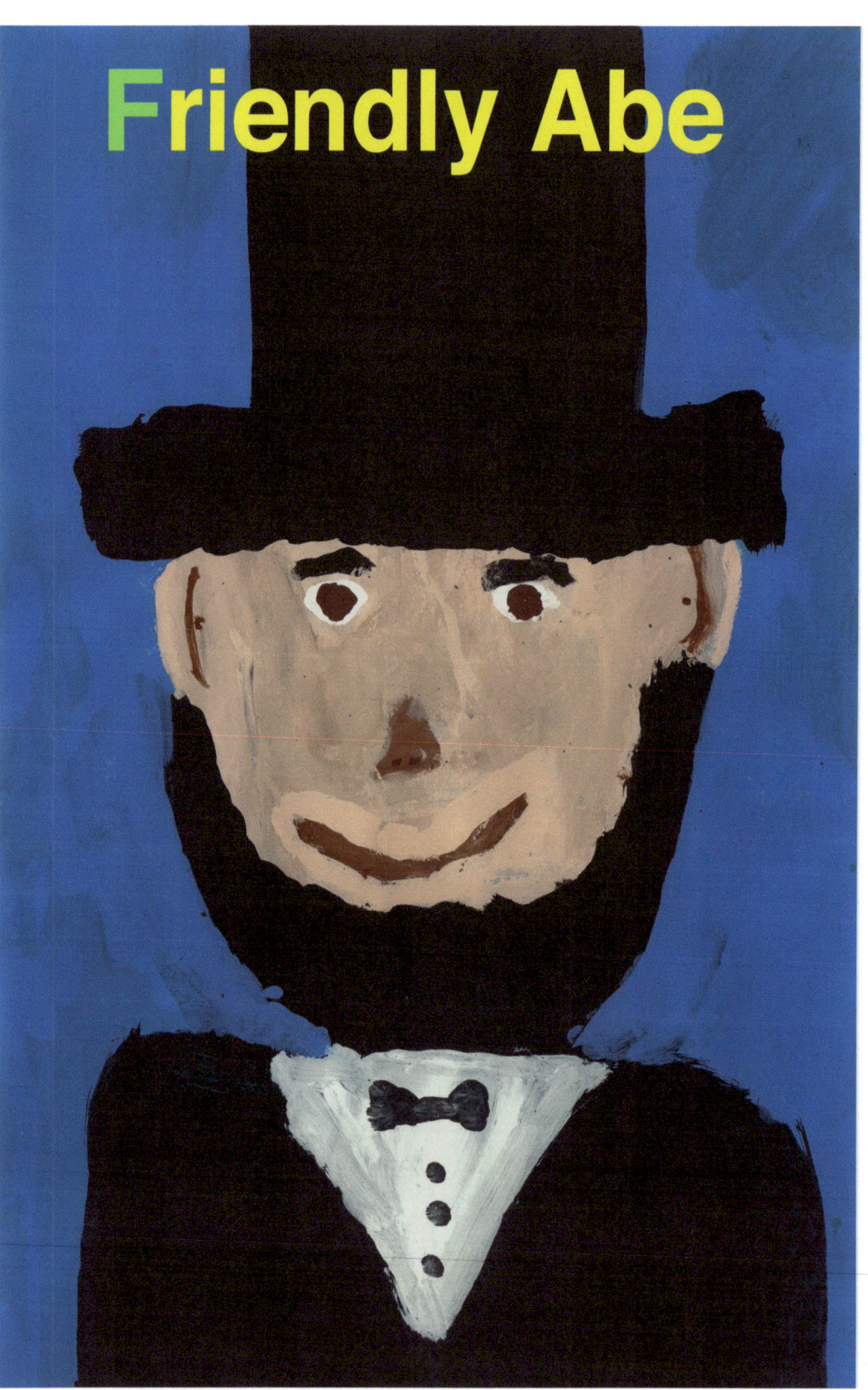

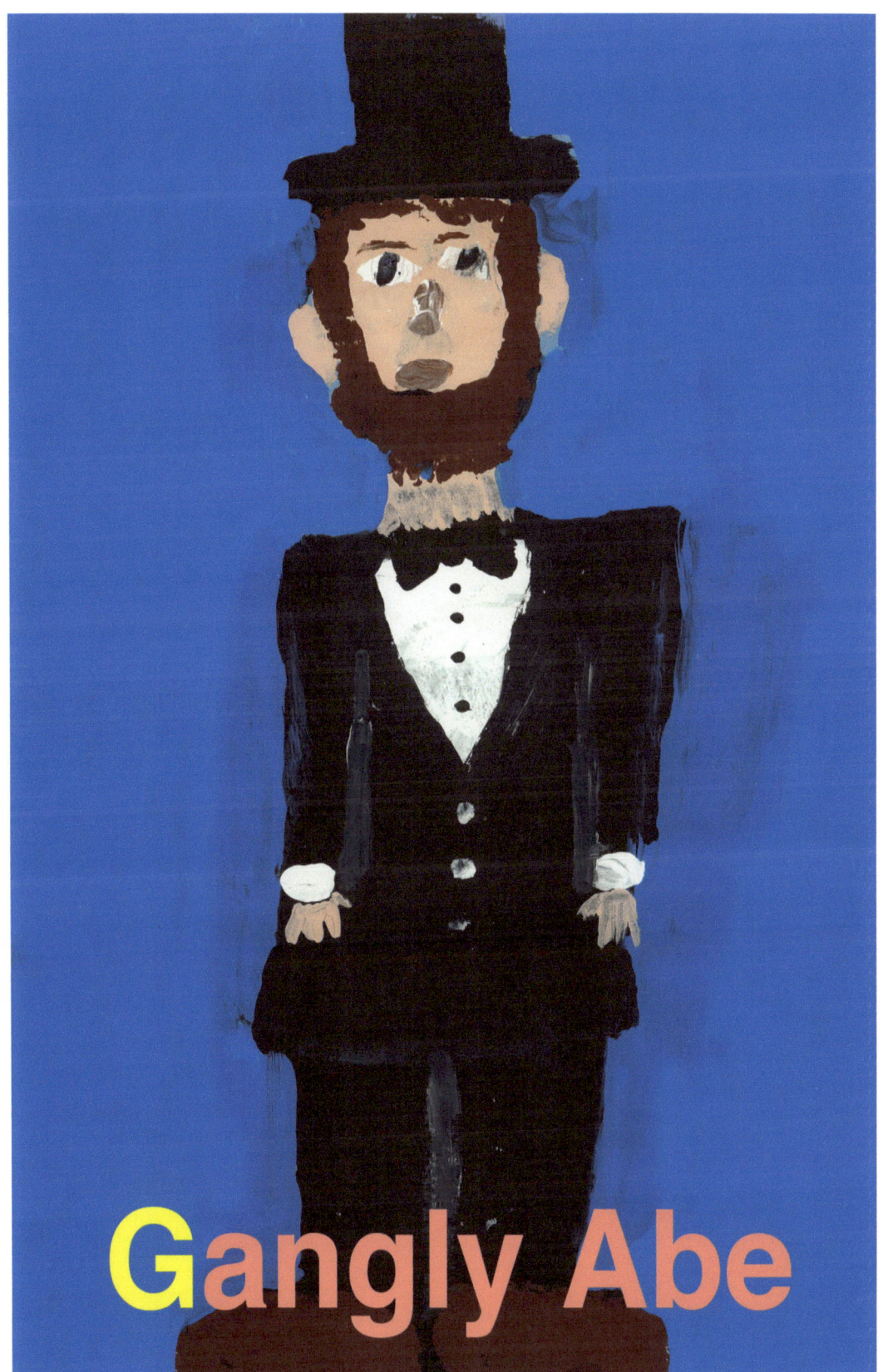

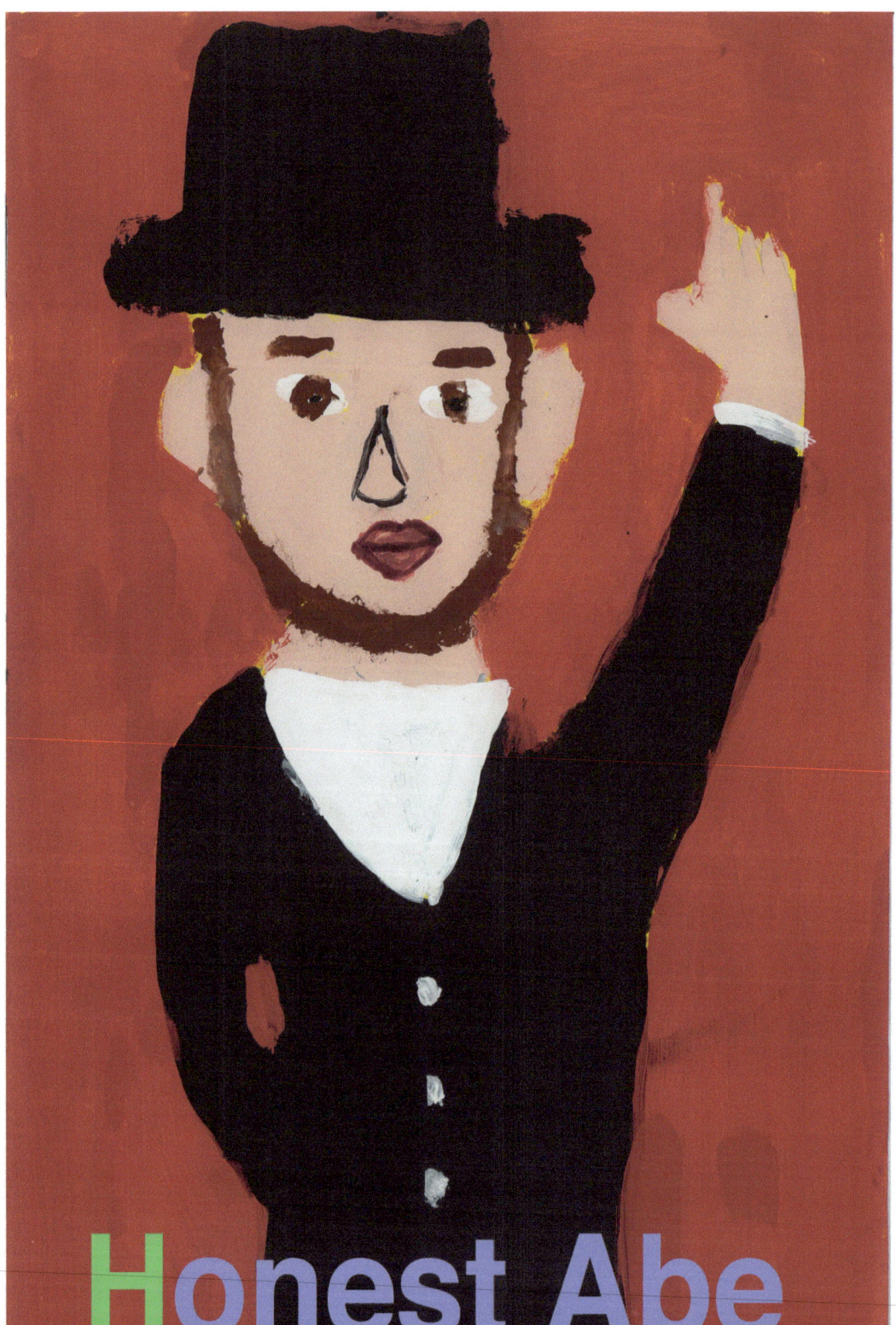

Honest Abe

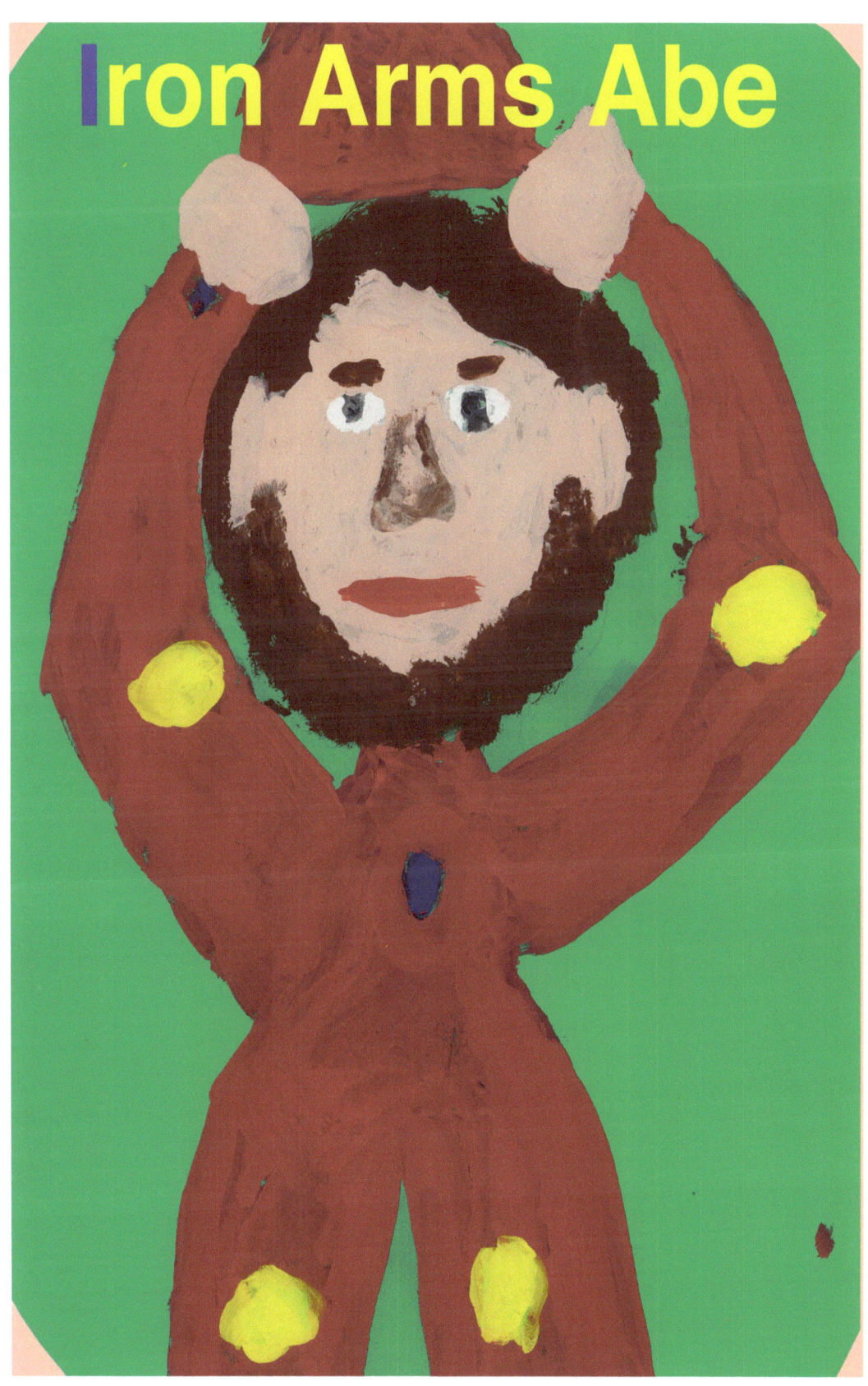

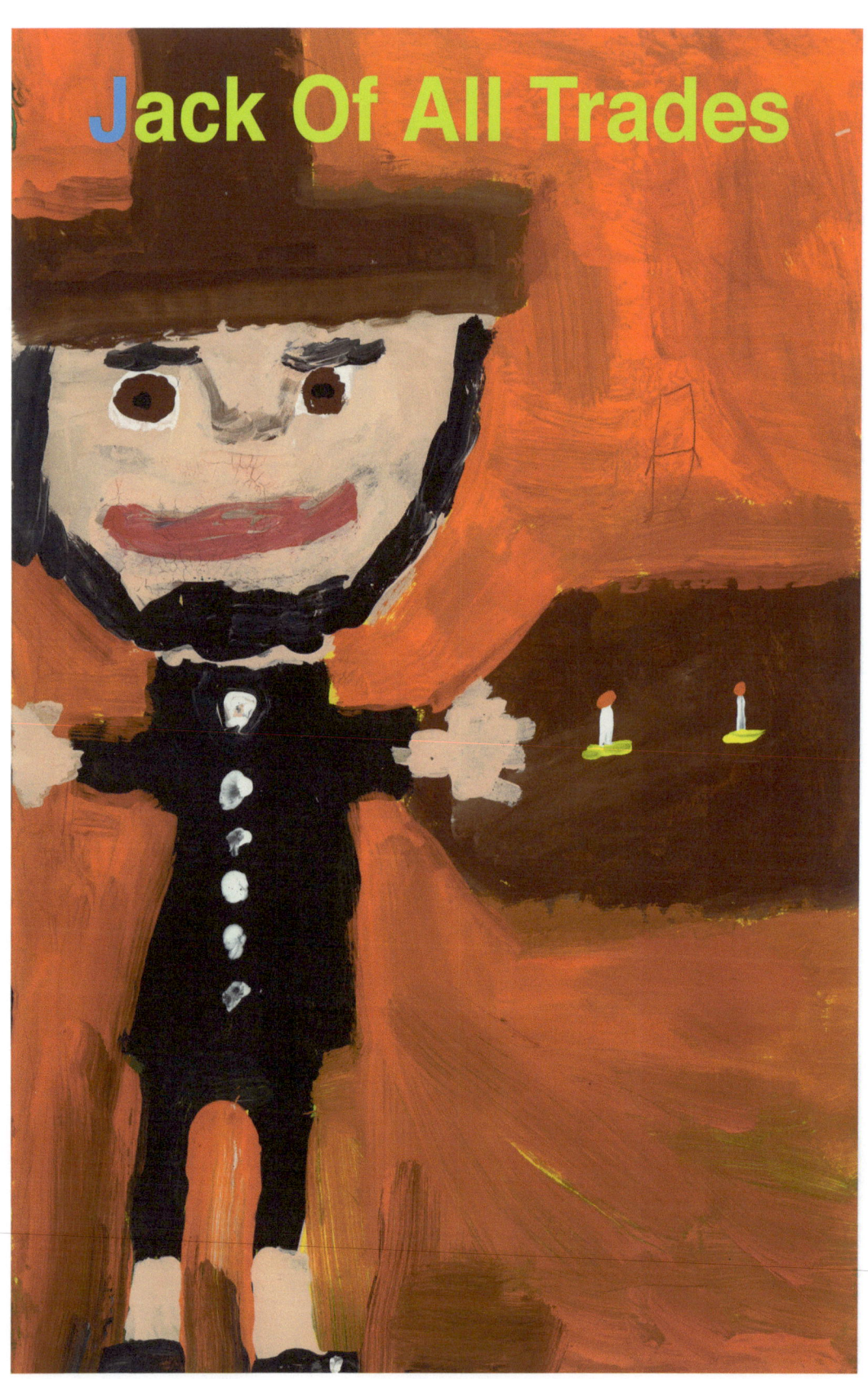

Jack Of All Trades

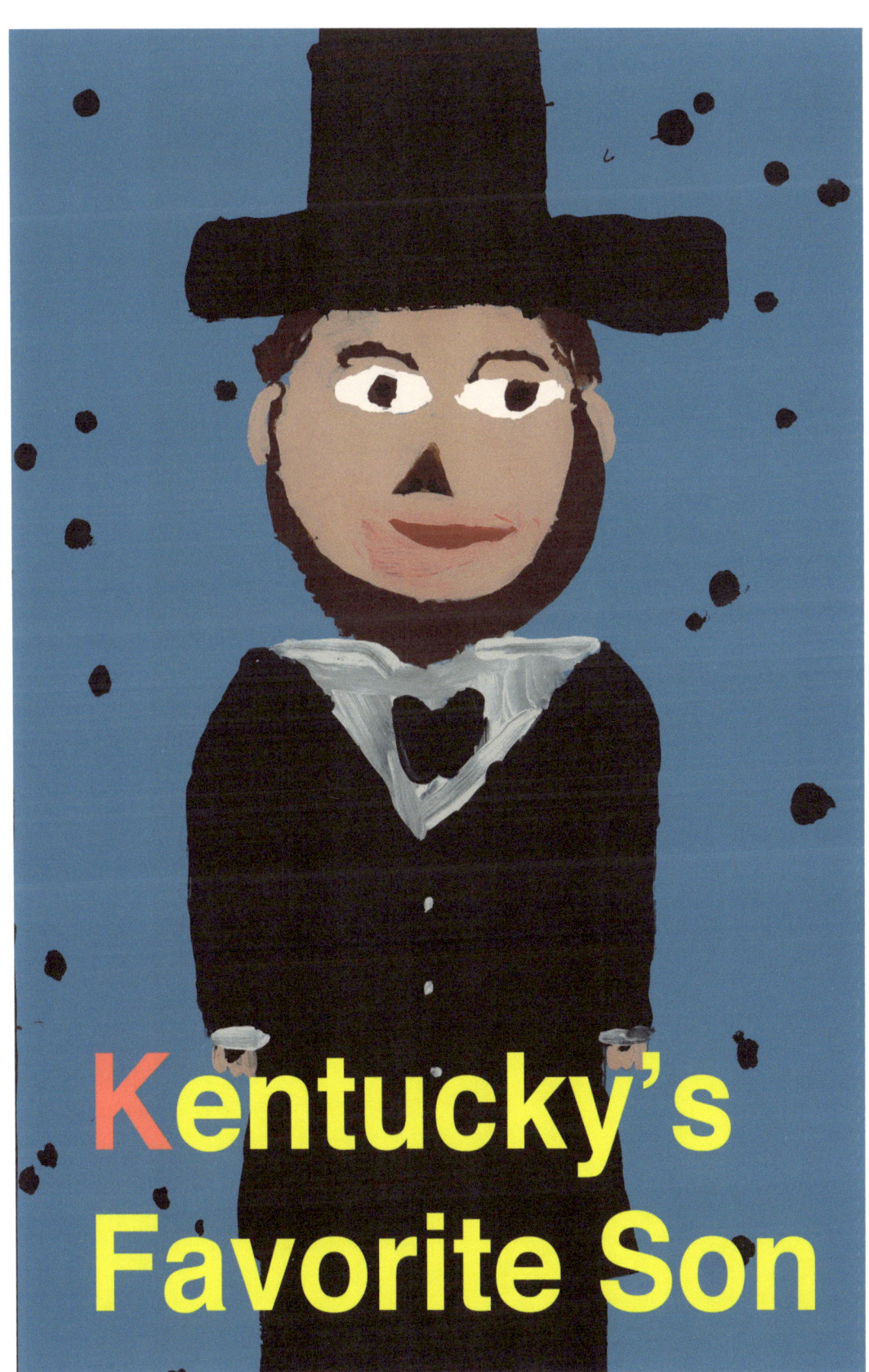

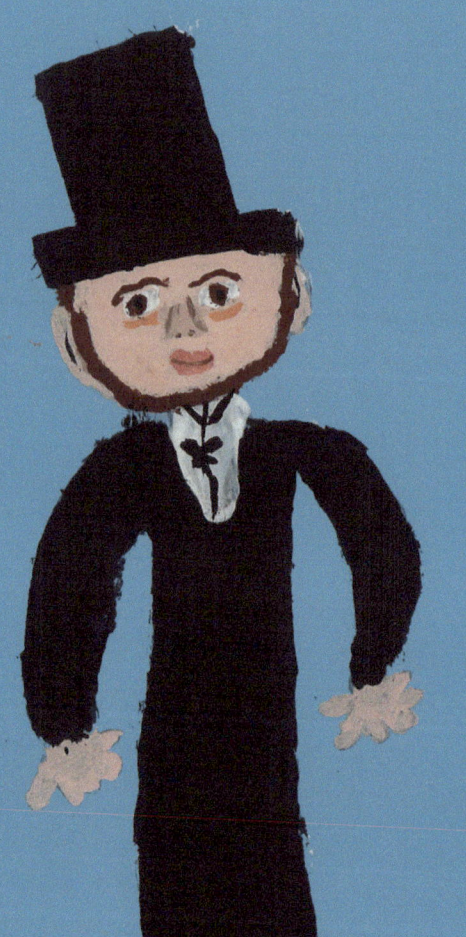

Lanky Lincoln

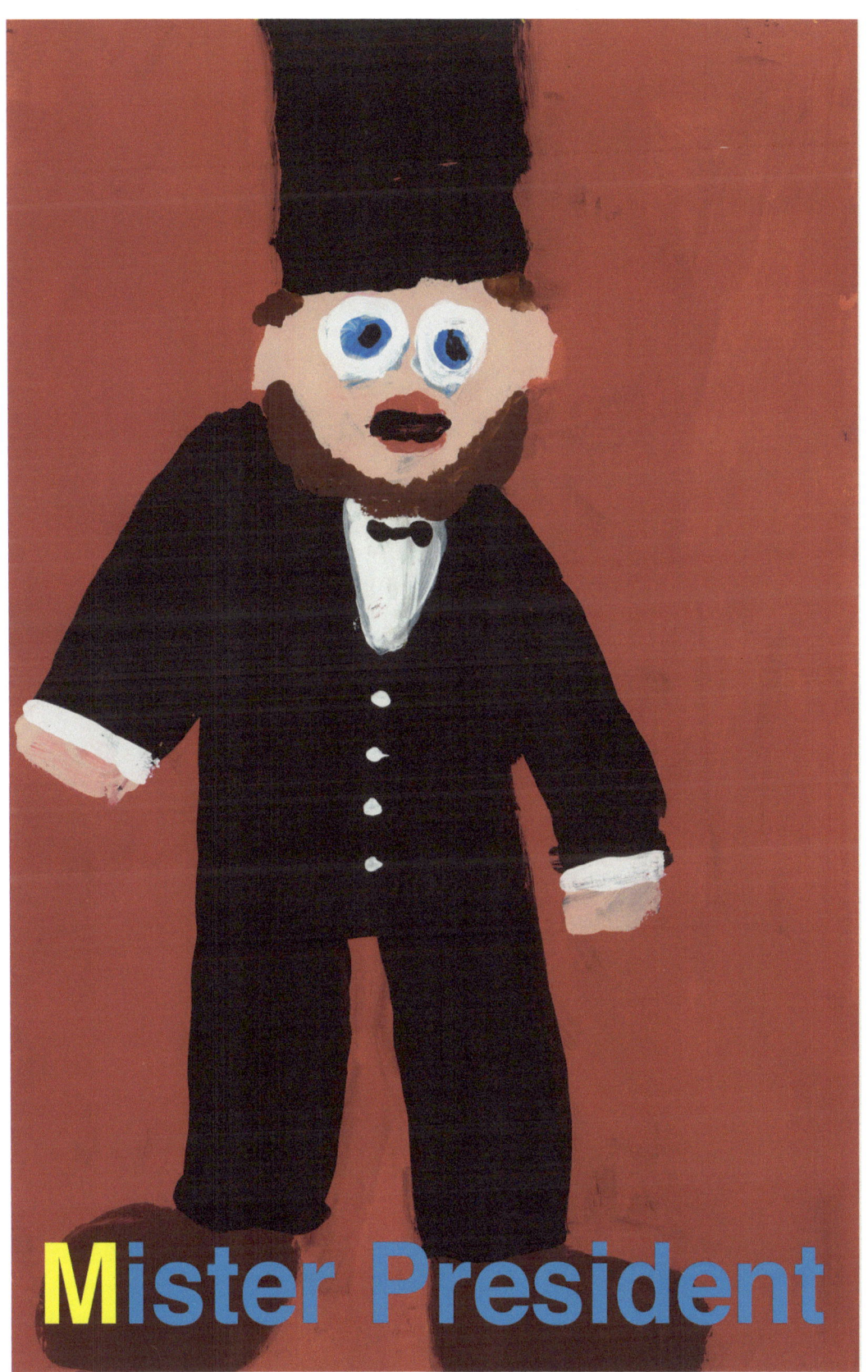

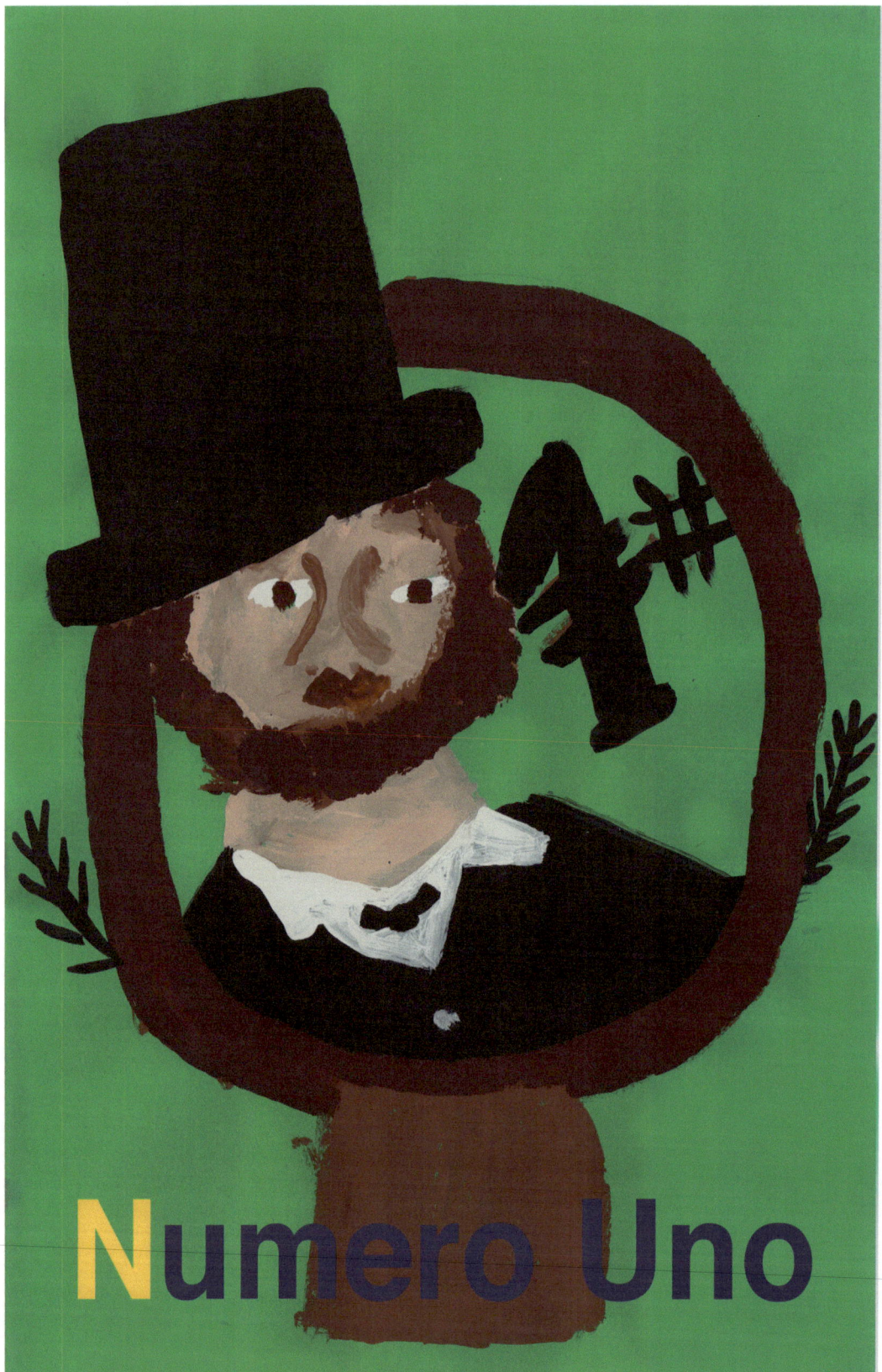

Numero Uno

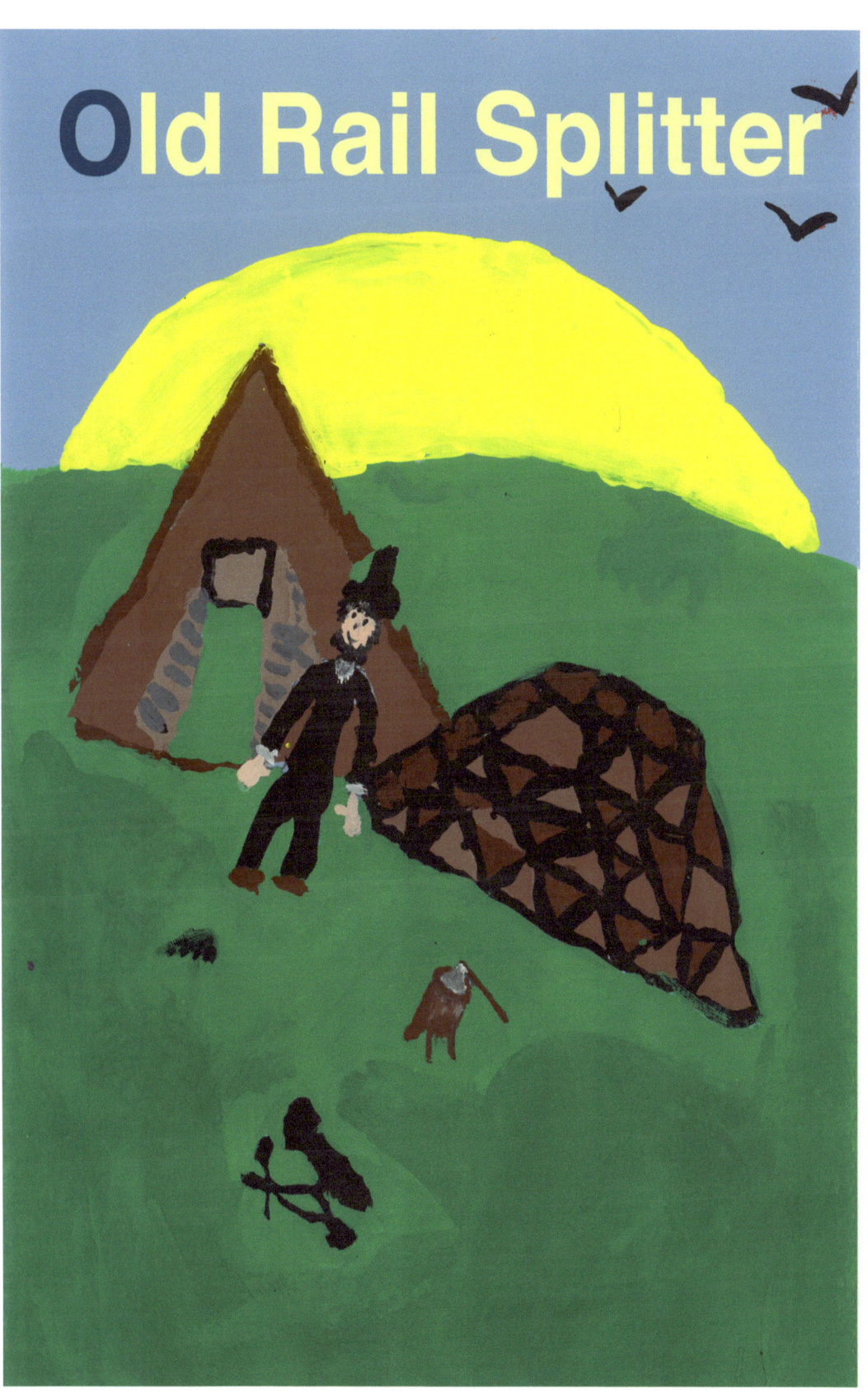

Professor-Walk-Six-Miles-To-Return-A-Book

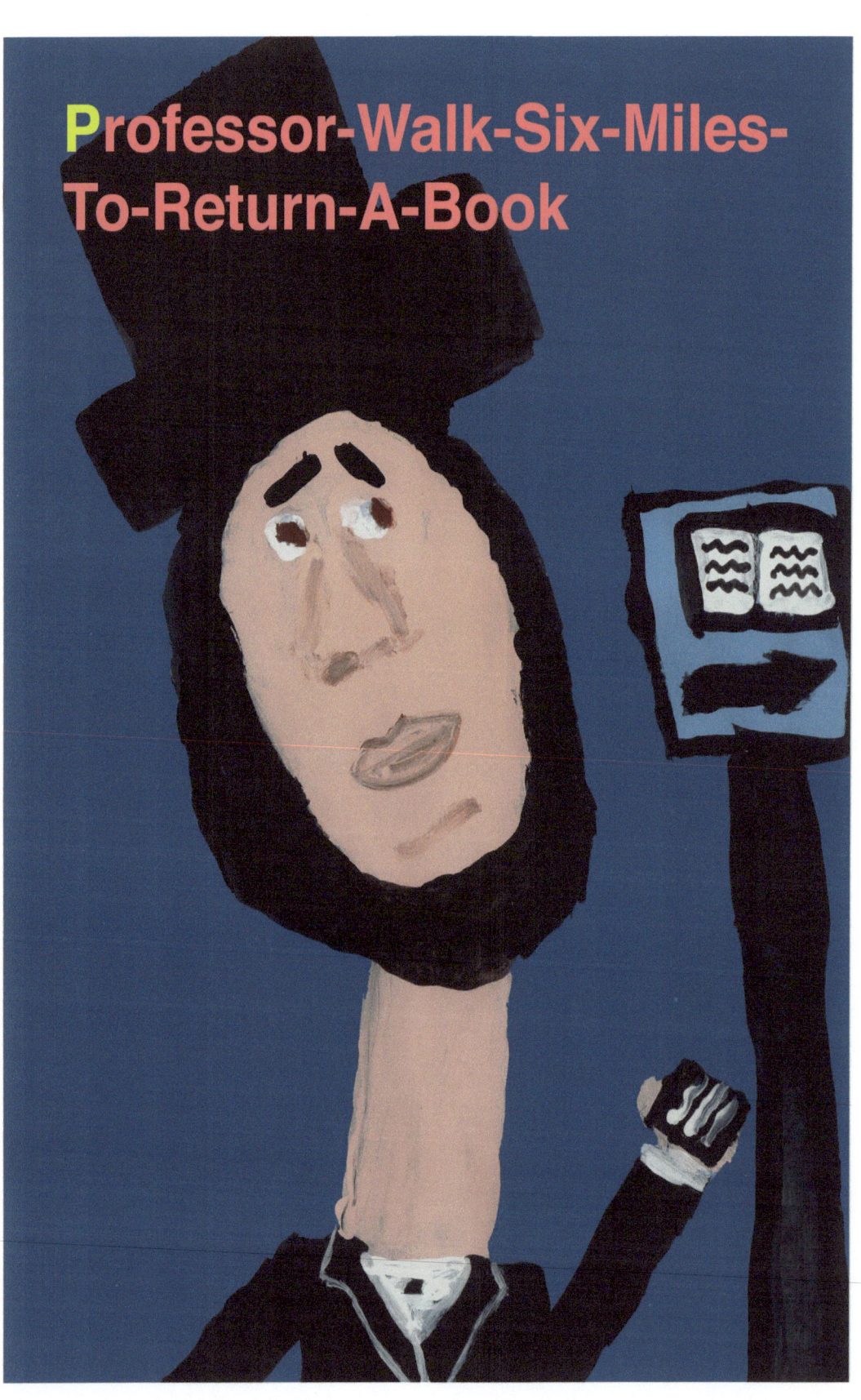

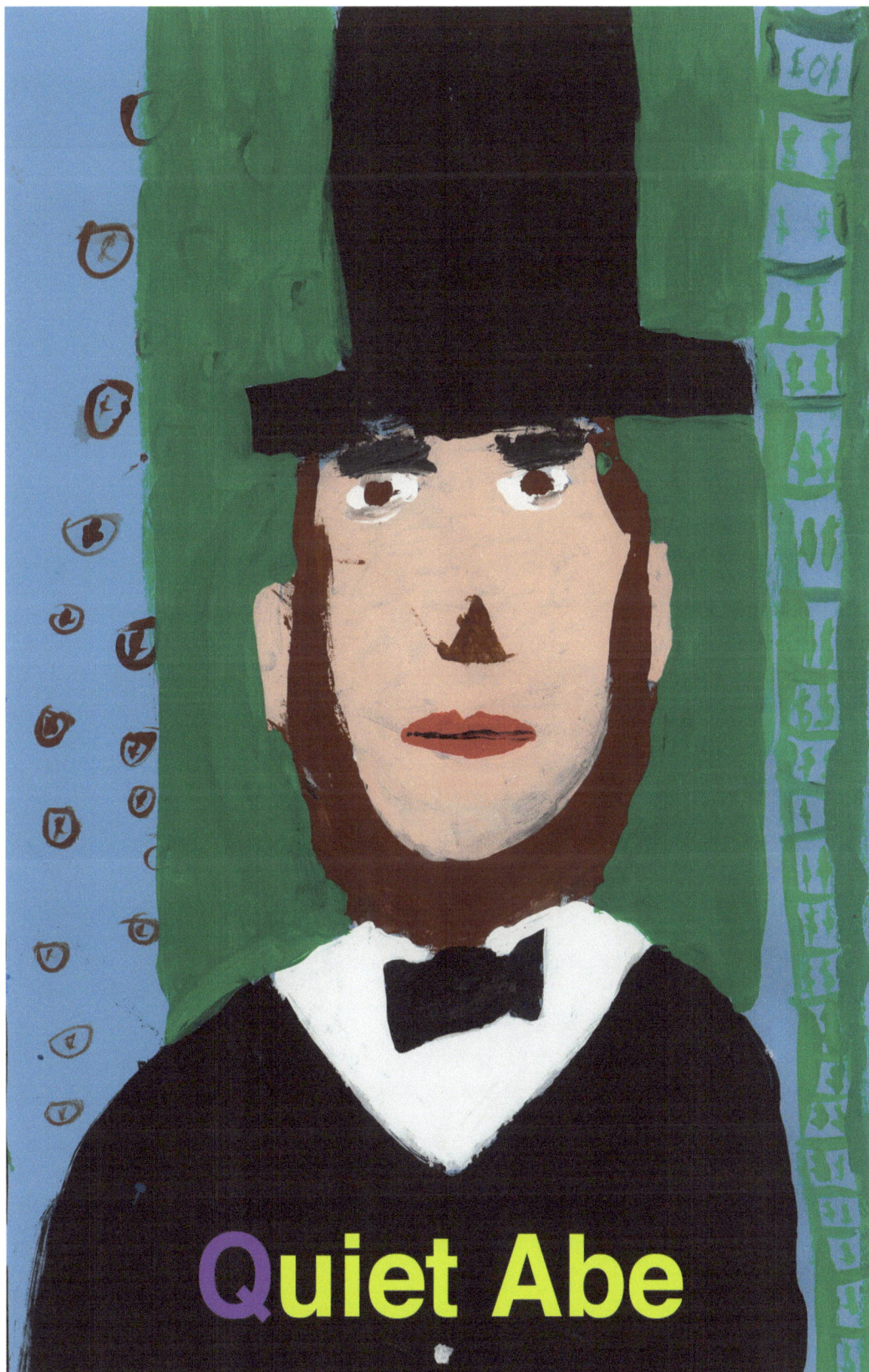

Quiet Abe

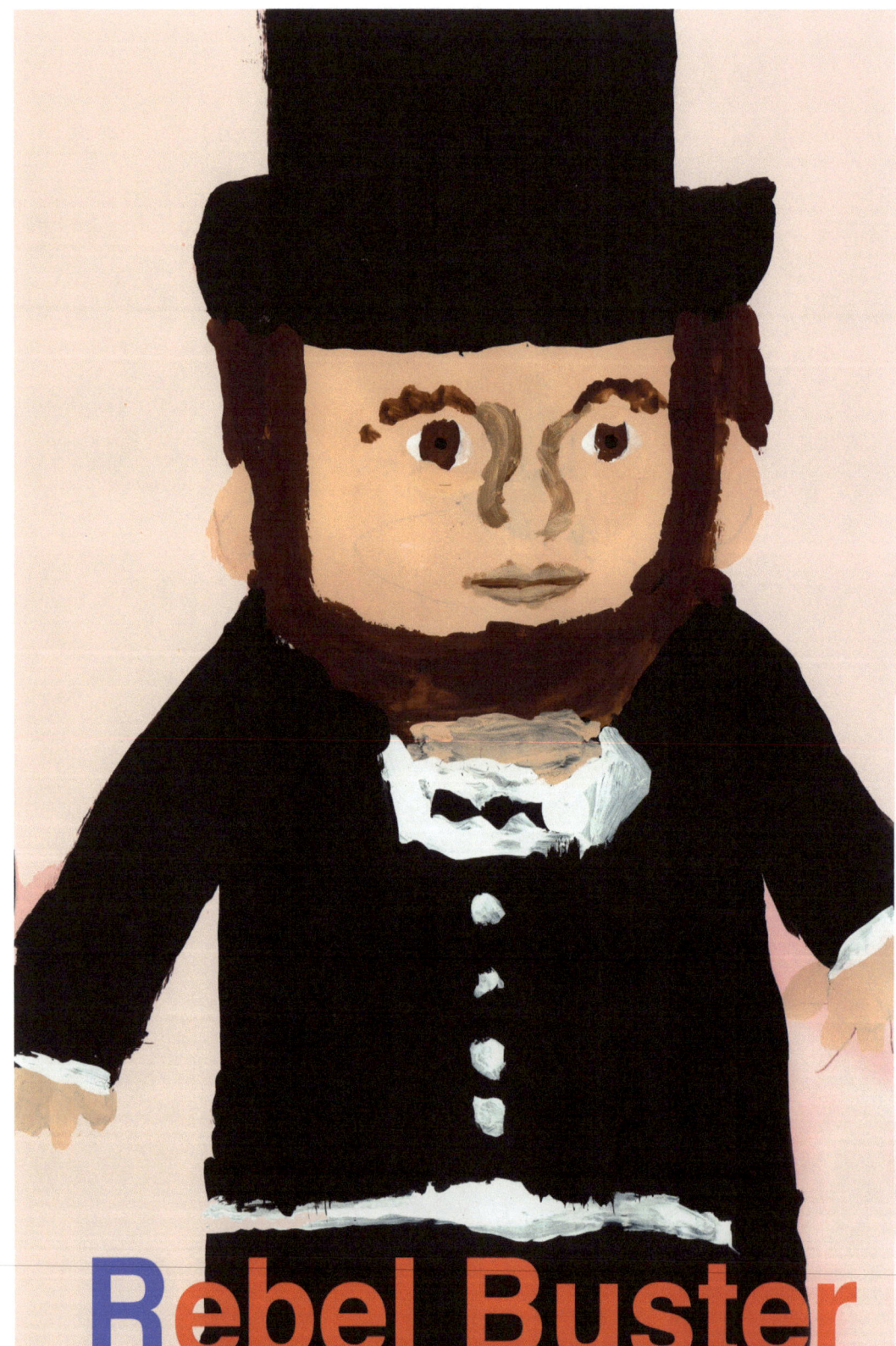

Rebel Buster

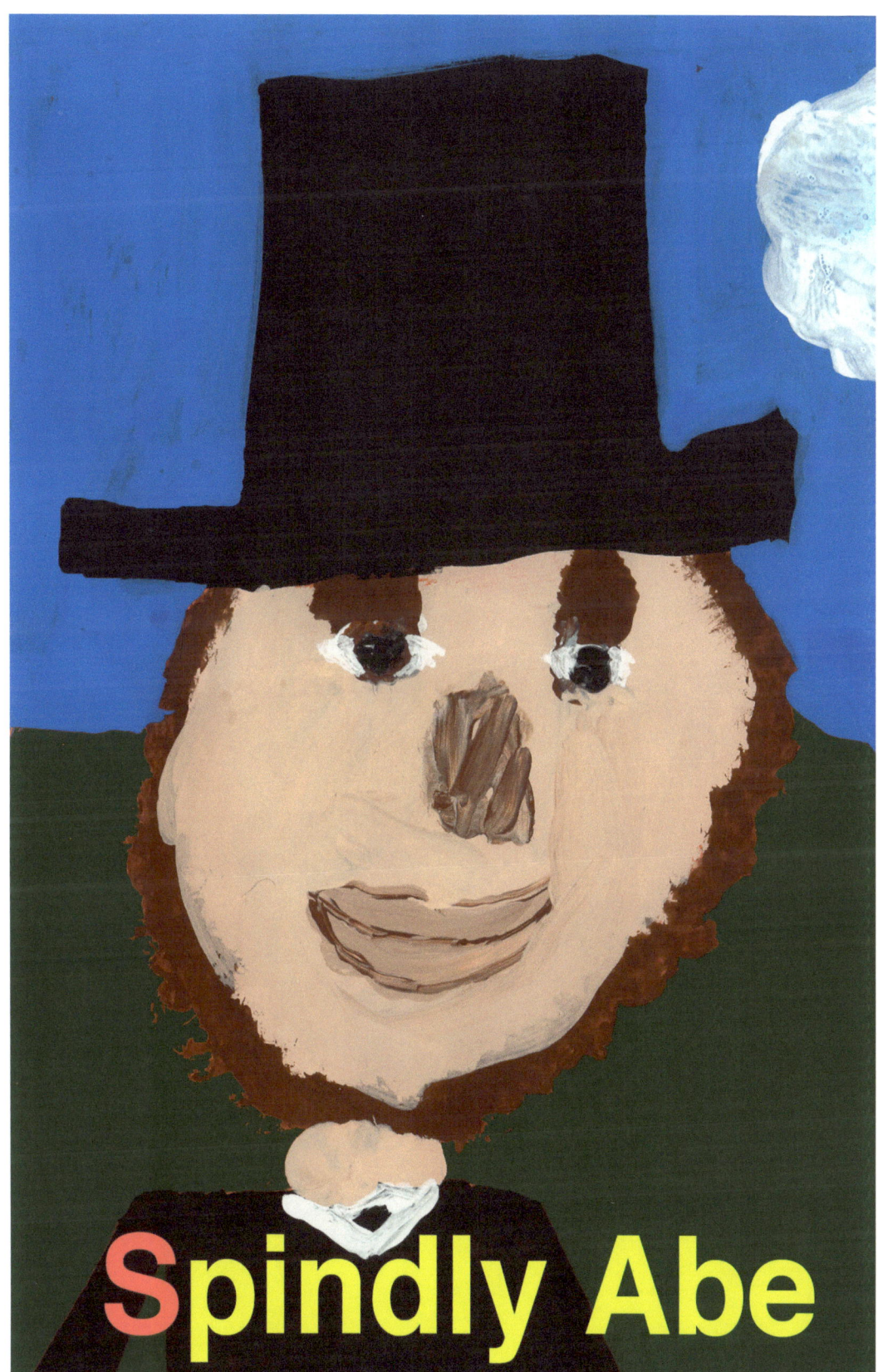

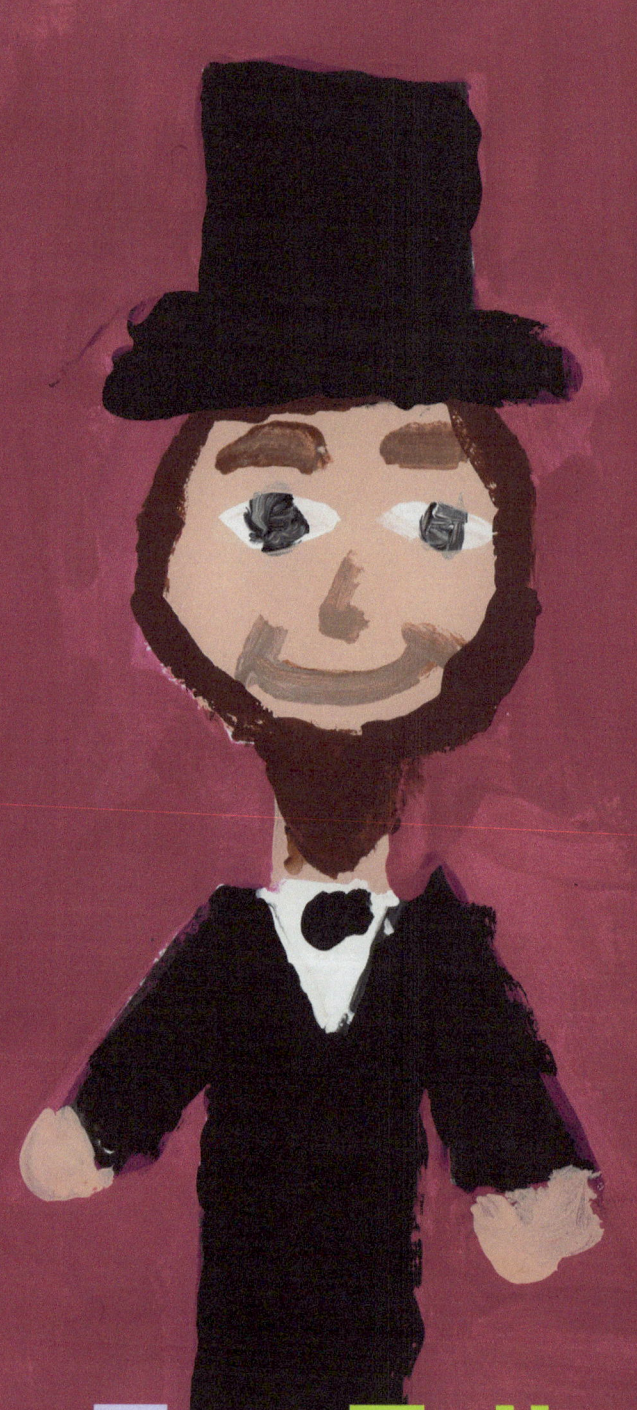

Too Tall

Uncle President

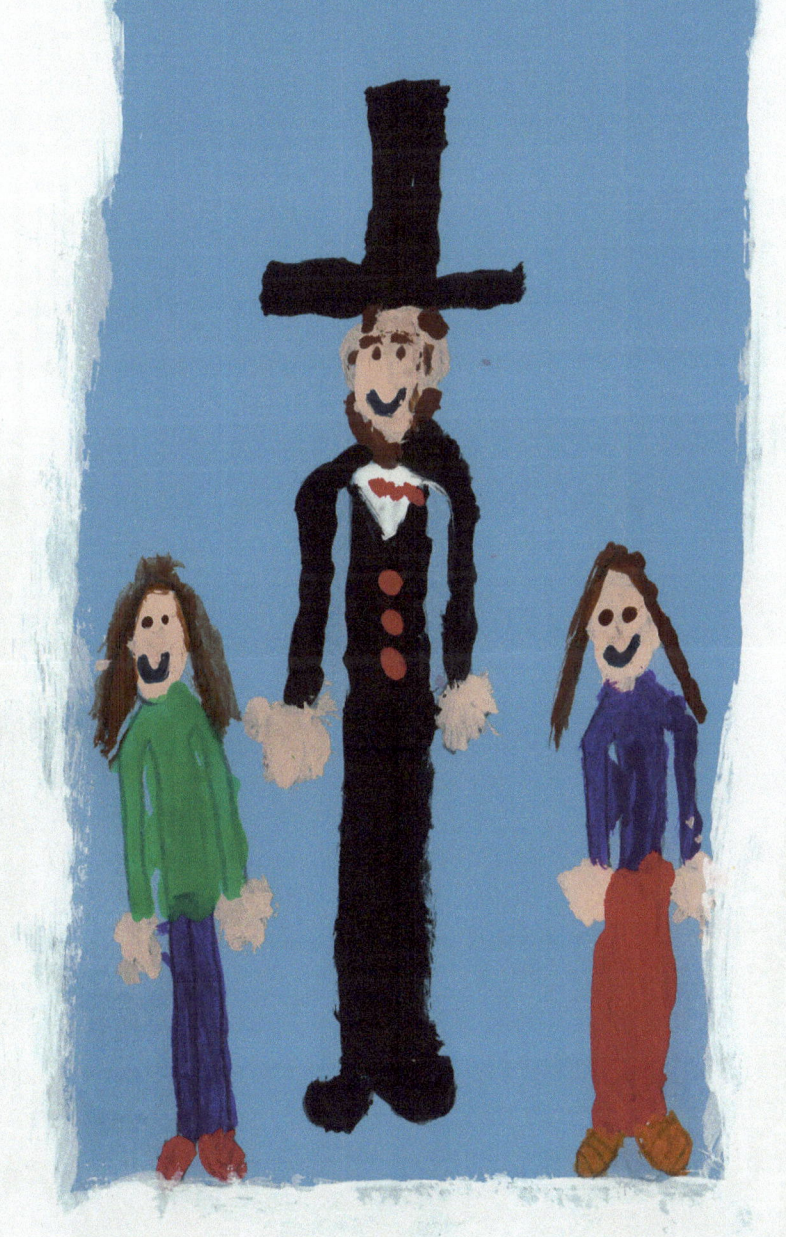

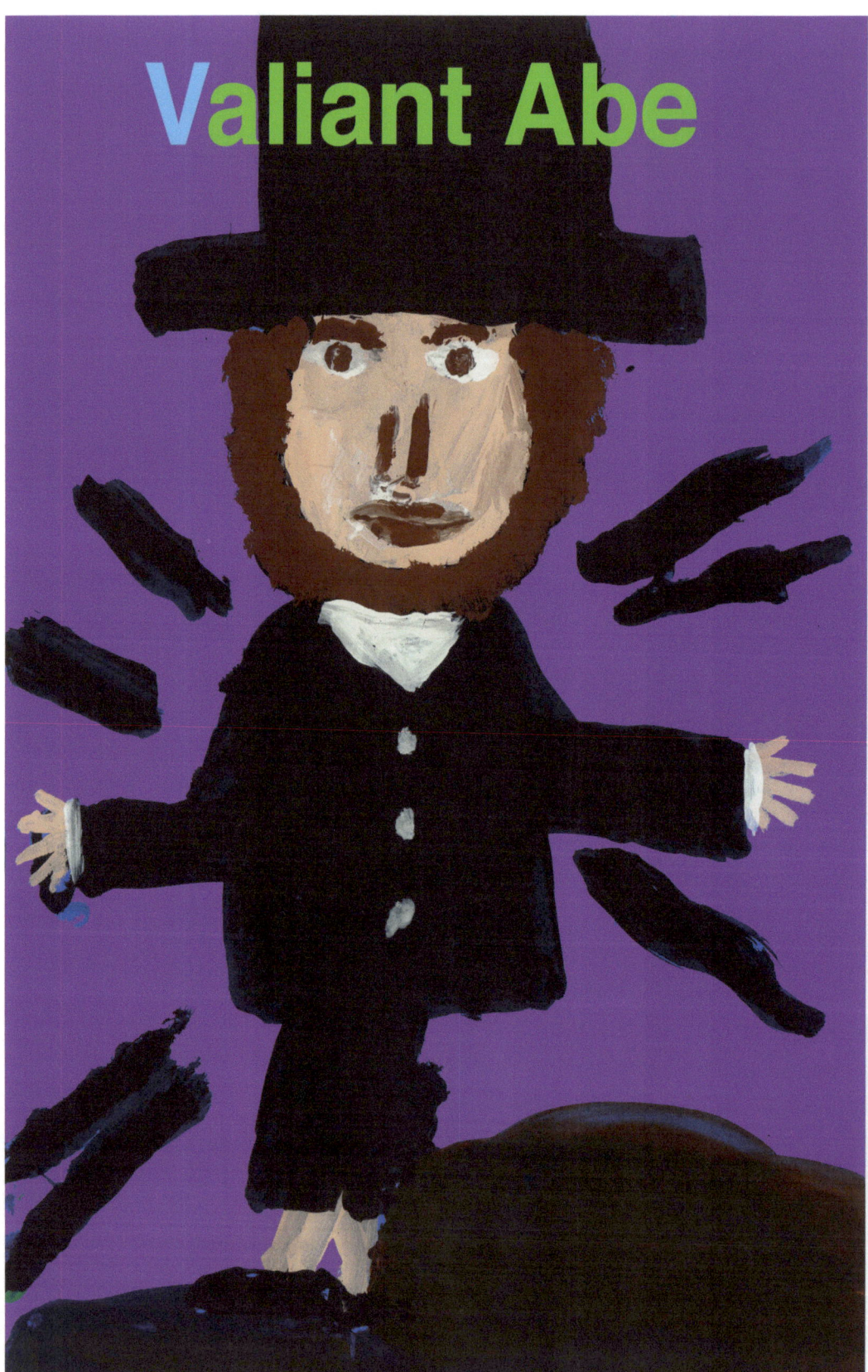

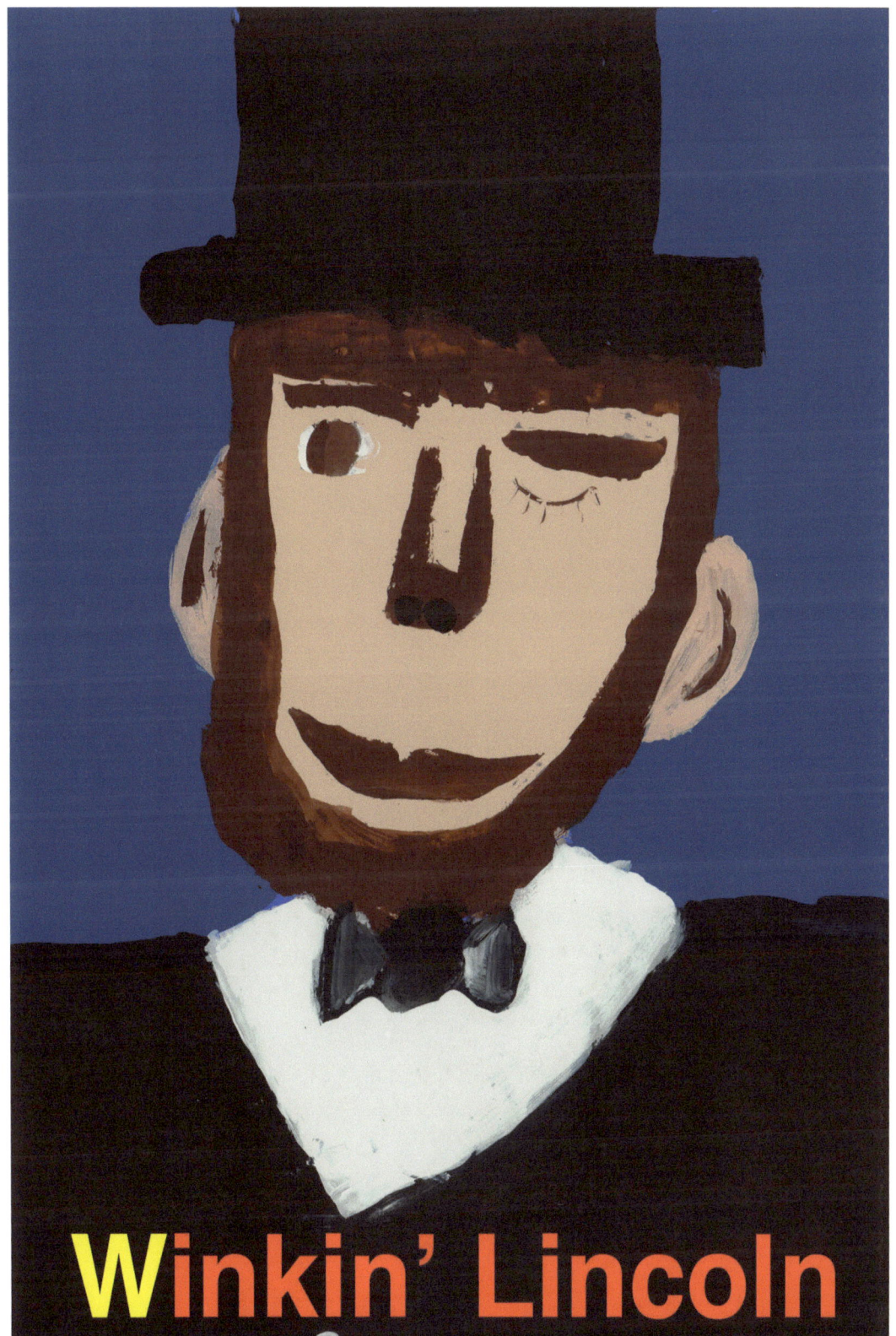

Mister X

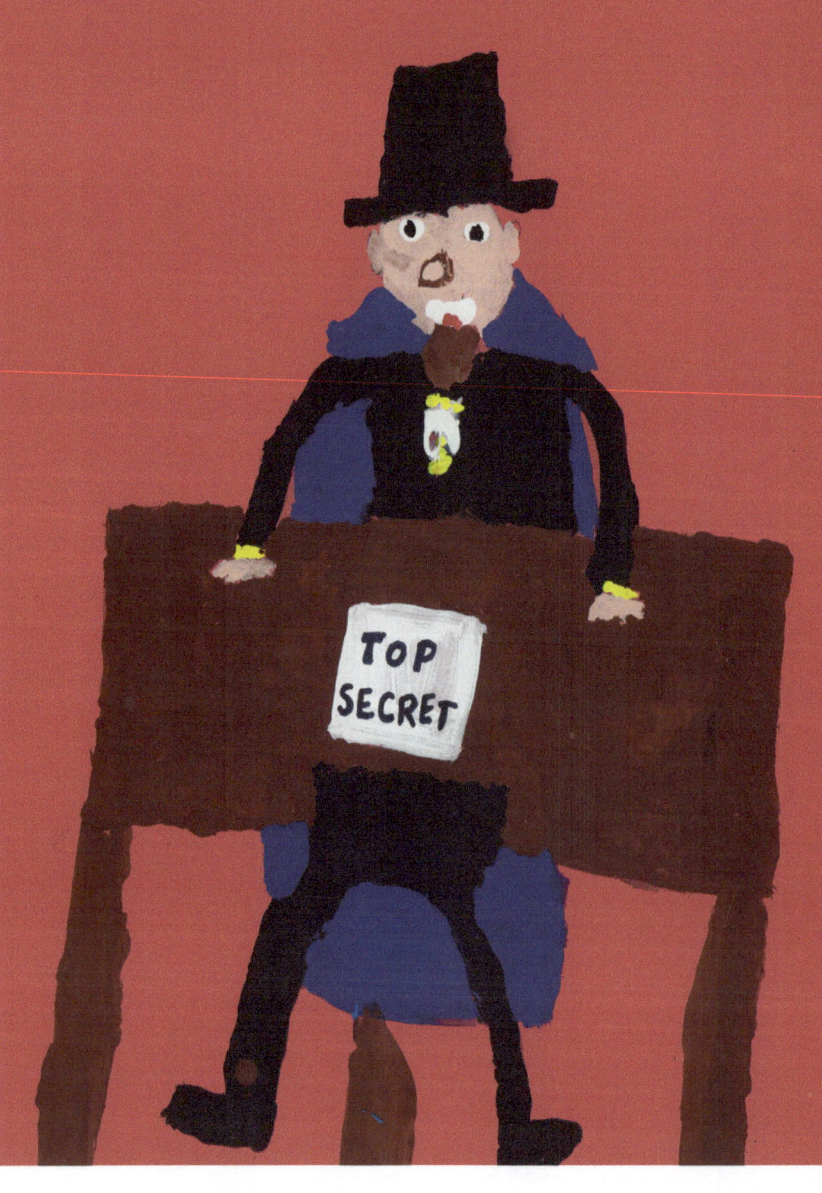

Young Abe Lincoln

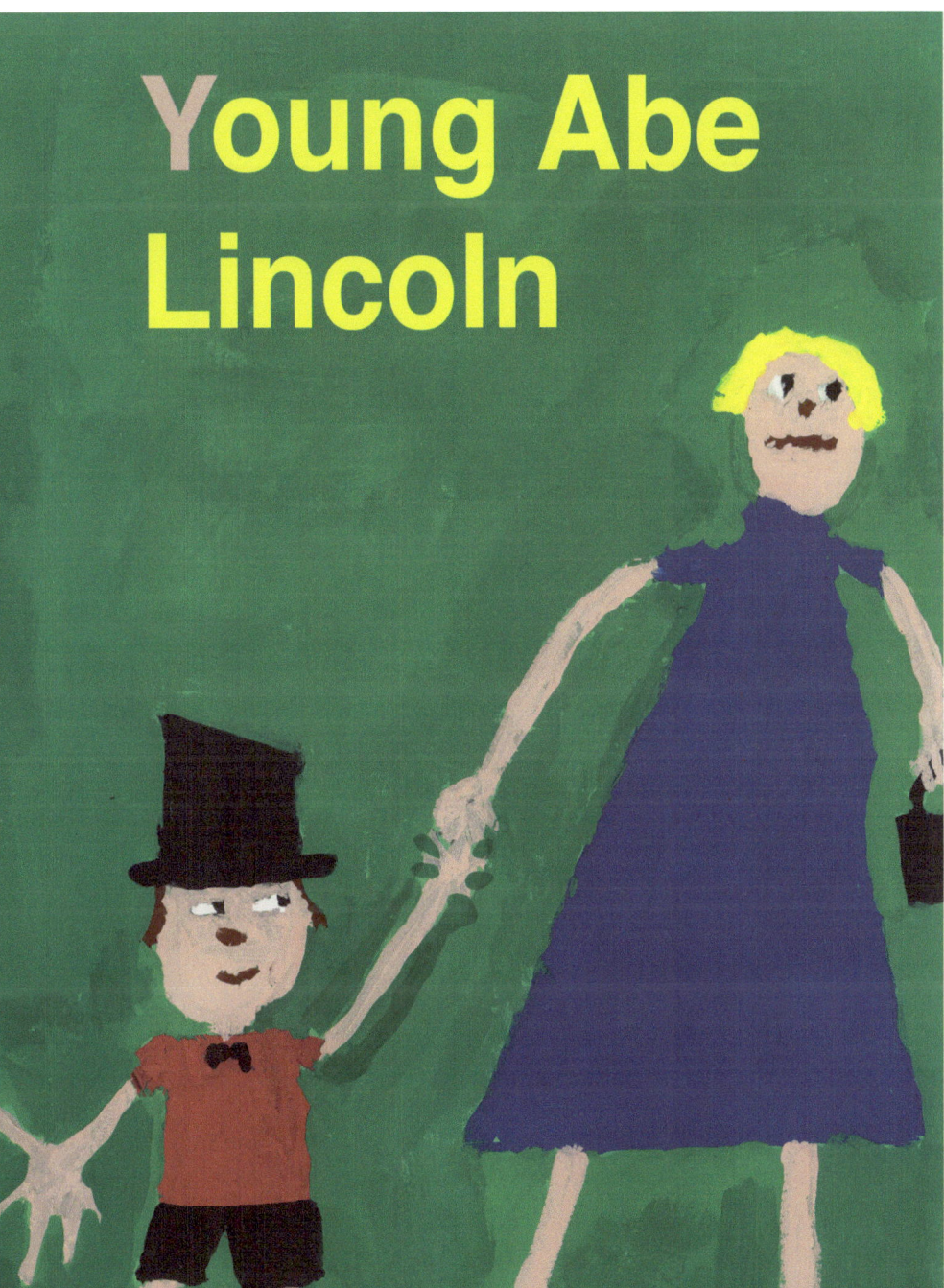

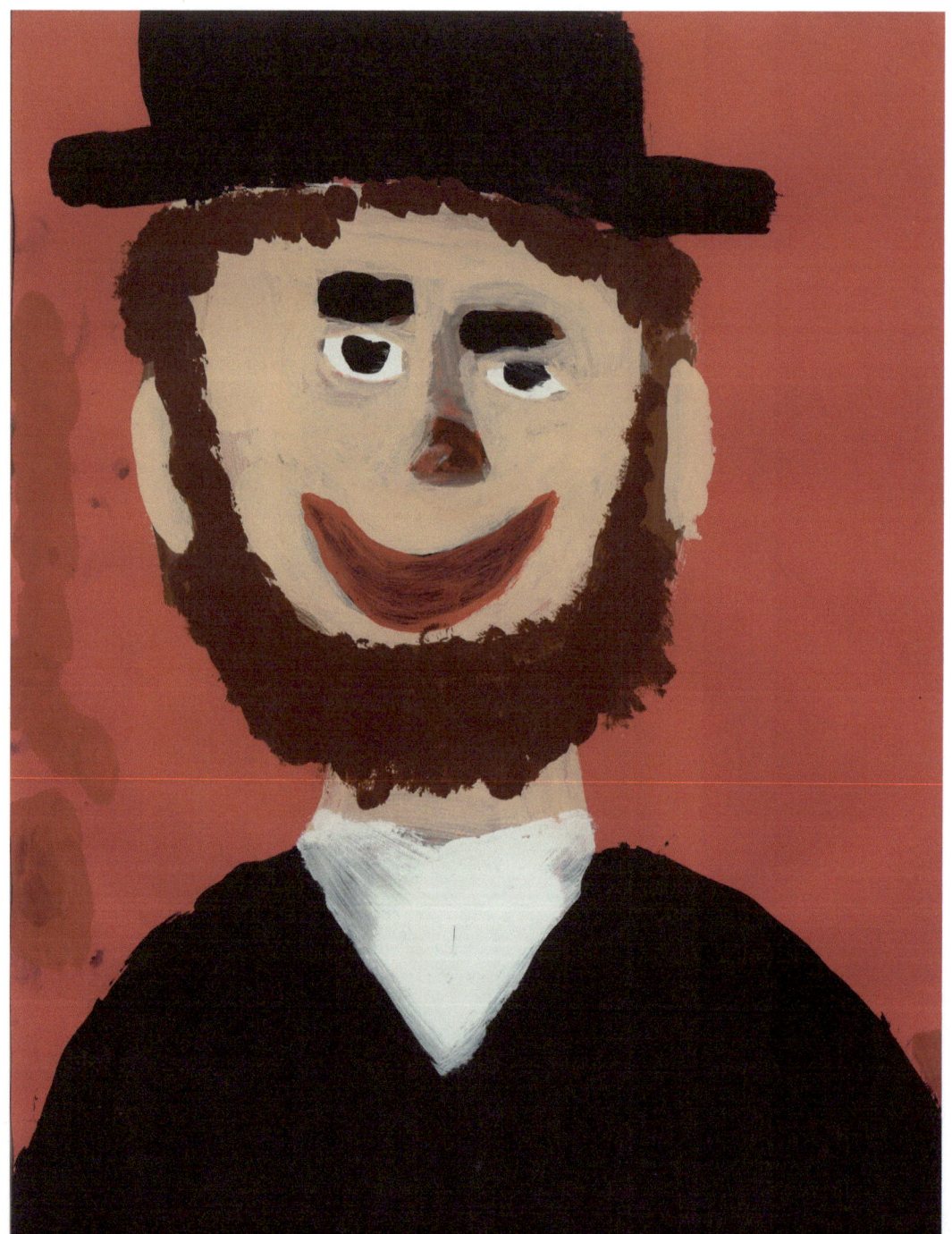

Zealous Abe

www.ingramcontent.com/pod-product-compliance
Lightning Source LLC
Chambersburg PA
CBHW041302180526
45172CB00003B/941